Sayyid Abul A'la

CH00924418

WITNESSES
UNTO
MANKIND

The Purpose and Duty of
the Muslim Ummah

Edited & Translated by
Khurram Murad

The Islamic Foundation

ISBN 978-0-86037-172-4 (PB)
ISBN 978-0-86037-173-1 (HB)

Editor: Khurram Murad

Cover design: Rashid Rahman

Published by
The Islamic Foundation
Markfield Dawah Centre
Ratby Lane, Markfield
Leicester LE67 9RN, UK

Quran House, PO Box 30611,
Nairobi, Kenya

PMB 3193,
Kano, Nigeria

New and edited English translation of the Urdu *Shahādat Ḥaq* (Lahore, 1947), which has previously been translated and published as the *Evidence of Truth* (Lahore, 1967).

British Library Cataloguing in Publication Data
  Mawdūdī, Sayyid Abūl A'la
    Witnesses unto mankind: the purpose and
    duty of the Muslim ummah.
    1. Islam
    I. Title II. Murad, Khurram
    III. Shahādat ḥaq. *English*
    297 BP161.2

ISBN 978-0-86037-173-1
ISBN 978-0-86037-172-4 Pb

Printed and bound by CPI Group (UK) Ltd, Croydon, CR0 4YY

بِسْمِ اللَّهِ الرَّحْمَٰنِ الرَّحِيمِ

يَٰٓأَيُّهَا ٱلَّذِينَ ءَامَنُوا ٱرْكَعُوا وَٱسْجُدُوا وَٱعْبُدُوا

رَبَّكُمْ وَٱفْعَلُوا ٱلْخَيْرَ لَعَلَّكُمْ تُفْلِحُونَ ۩ ۝٧٧

وَجَٰهِدُوا فِي ٱللَّهِ حَقَّ جِهَادِهِ هُوَ ٱجْتَبَىٰكُمْ وَمَا جَعَلَ

عَلَيْكُمْ فِي ٱلدِّينِ مِنْ حَرَجٍ مِّلَّةَ أَبِيكُمْ إِبْرَٰهِيمَ هُوَ سَمَّىٰكُمُ

ٱلْمُسْلِمِينَ مِن قَبْلُ وَفِي هَٰذَا لِيَكُونَ ٱلرَّسُولُ شَهِيدًا عَلَيْكُمْ

وَتَكُونُوا شُهَدَآءَ عَلَى ٱلنَّاسِ فَأَقِيمُوا ٱلصَّلَوٰةَ وَءَاتُوا ٱلزَّكَوٰةَ

وَٱعْتَصِمُوا بِٱللَّهِ هُوَ مَوْلَىٰكُمْ فَنِعْمَ ٱلْمَوْلَىٰ وَنِعْمَ ٱلنَّصِيرُ ۝٧٨

سُورَةُ الْحَجِّ ٢٢

In the Name of God,
the Most Gracious, the Most Merciful

O believers, bow down and prostrate yourselves, and serve only your Lord, and do good, so that you might attain well-being. And struggle in the way of God as ought to be struggled in His way. He has chosen you, and He has not laid on you in your Din any constriction. Follow the way of your father, Abraham. He has named you Muslims, before and in this, so that the Messenger would be a witness before you, and you would be witnesses before all mankind. So establish the Prayer, give the Alms, and hold fast unto God. He is your Master. How excellent the Master, and how excellent the Helper.

(al-Ḥajj 22: 77–8)

Contents

Foreword

Witnesses unto Mankind: The Purpose and Duty of the Muslim Ummah is a new and edited English translation of Sayyid Abul A'la Mawdudi's (1903–1979) *Shahādat Ḥaq* in Urdu. It contains an address which he delivered on 30 December, 1946 at a regional conference of the Jama'at Islami, Lahore Division, held at Muradpur, Sialkot, then in pre-partition India, now in Pakistan.*

Published immediately afterwards, *Shahādat Ḥaq* has since been reprinted many times, both separately and as a part of a larger collection of Sayyid Mawdudi's works, *Islam kā Niẓām Zindigī* (Lahore, 1962), by commercial publishers and by friends and admirers who desired to disseminate its important message on a larger scale. It has also been translated into several languages, the first English translation appearing under the title the *Evidence of Truth* (Lahore, 1967). Now, this entirely new and more extended English version is being published by the Islamic Foundation.

The message and substance of Sayyid Mawdudi's address is of fundamental importance both to Muslims and to mankind at large, as the English title adopted by me shows. Put simply: Muslims, who now constitute one-fifth of the human race, have no other justification to exist as a community but that they should bear witness, before mankind, to

---

* The Jama'at Islami was formed as a result of Sayyid Mawdudi's call, in Lahore, now in Pakistan, on 2 Sha'ban 1360/26 August, 1941, in a gathering of about 75 persons. Sayyid Mawdudi was elected its first Amir.

9

the Truth and guidance which God has given them. For this very purpose, he explains, God sent all the Prophets. They showed man the right way of life, the path of his Creator, so that he could live by it and not plead ignorance when called to account on the Day of Judgement. After the Last Prophet, blessings and peace be on him, it is Muslims who must fulfil this prophetic mission to all mankind and for all times to come.

Describing how this witness must be given, both by words and deeds, Sayyid Mawdudi proceeds to depict how the Muslims' words and deeds have in fact become witnesses against Islam. Their failure to do their duty and, instead, giving false witness, he holds, is the sole cause of their present state of ignominy and backwardness. Later, he also explains that the Jama'at Islami was formed precisely to do this duty and invite all Muslims to it. Finally, he answers certain objections which were then being raised against the Jama'at Islami.

His style, as usual, possesses all the directness and clarity, the passionate lucidity, and the persuasive logic, so characteristic of him.* Because of its message and style, this brief booklet has made a deep impact on its readers, and stirred many people to renew their commitment to Allah and come forward to fulfil their covenant with Him.

Though delivered about four decades ago in a party conference, Sayyid Mawdudi's message is universal and timeless. The need to hear it remains as great as ever. But the presently available English translation retains little of the charm and power that characterize the original Urdu work. Hence it has not been able to penetrate the hearts and minds of English readers as it should have. The need for a better English translation was, therefore, great. English is now spoken by millions of Muslims, who can all benefit immensely from an improved English version. I hope that this new translation will bring them, in some degree, nearer

---

* See my Introductions to his *The Islamic Movement: Dynamics of Values, Power and Change* (Leicester, 1984) and *Let Us Be Muslims* (Leicester, 1985).

to the life and power that fill Sayyid Mawdudi's original words.

The editorial work, in addition to contributing an introduction and notes containing Quranic references, has been confined to providing necessary headings and sub-headings, incorporating certain footnotes in the text, and removing the last part, dealing with the objections against the Jama'at Islami, to an appendix at the end of the book.

The extensive references from the Qur'ān that I have provided should prove an important addition. What need do they fulfil? Firstly, the Qur'ān is the source of Sayyid Mawdudi's message and argument. Hence these notes should help the reader to discover how both are linked. Secondly, as I have written elsewhere, I expect that this work will continue to be used, as it has been so far, by the generations of Muslims who are ardently striving to make their lives Islamic. In many groups, study circles, classes and organizations around the world, it will be eagerly taken up as a basic text. It is most essential, however, that all studies on Islam are pursued, as far as possible, within the framework of the Qur'ān and Hadith. To these the Muslim youth, intelligentsia and scholars must turn again and again and draw closer and closer. I sincerely hope that my notes will serve as a means towards that end, and that they will encourage the reader into a more direct intimate relationship with the Qur'ān.

It is my earnest hope that this book will stir the hearts of its readers and inspire them to take up the challenge that Sayyid Mawdudi has placed before them. I also pray to Allah, subhanahu wata'ala, to bless this effort with His forgiveness, mercy and acceptance.

Leicester   **Khurram Murad**
16 December, 1985
3 Jumada 'l-Ula, 1406

Introduction

by Khurram Murad

Shahadah in Islamic Life and Discourse

Shahādah, of which 'witness' is the English equivalent, is central to Islam. It is a fundamentally important key word in the Islamic vocabulary. It plays a crucial role in defining and shaping the Islamic life and discourse, a life and discourse which extends from the existential to the cosmic.

'Witnessing', thus, lies at the heart of Islam, it constitutes the precincts of Islam. One can enter Islam only upon saying the Shahadah, one can remain in Islam only by saying and doing the Shahadah. It is the first word that a new-born Muslim baby hears, it is the first and foremost of the pillars of Islam on which he constructs and sustains the entire edifice of his Islamic life, it must be the last word on his lips as he departs from this world to meet his Maker. Five times a day it must be proclaimed to the world from minarets and rooftops wherever a Muslim might happen to be; still much more often it must be uttered in the deep silence of the heart. In between, every aspect of his life should be shaped by the Shahadah.

And, finally, by voluntarily laying down his life in the way of God, he deserves to be called a *shahīd*, a witness *par excellence* to his faith and the Truth he has received. It is also interesting to note here that the English word 'martyr', too, etymologically means 'witness', or *shahīd*. First used in

13

Christianity for those who were put to death in the cause of their faith, it provides strong evidence that the link between faith and witness is common to all faiths, for all of them originated from one source and were centred on commitment to the One God.

Witness to what? To the Truth. But what does the Truth mean?

The Arabic word *al-ḥaqq*, which has been translated as the 'Truth', is used in the Qur'ān in a number of ways: justification, moral or legal (2: 61); right, as against wrong (13: 17); right and due (2: 180, 17: 26, 3: 102); purpose and meaning (6: 73, 44: 39); certain, real and true (6: 62, 7: 8, 31: 30, 45: 32).

Obviously, God is *the* ultimate and most certain reality and truth (24: 25, 10: 32); indeed, in a sense, only He is Real and True, because all else exist only because of Him. Therefore His guidance, too, by which He guides man – and only He can so guide (10: 35) – to Himself and to the true knowledge of right and wrong in every respect is the Truth. Hence, the Truth means the Divine guidance in this pervasive sense, as given by God through His Messengers and Books, and, finally, through the Qur'ān and the Last Prophet, Muhammad, blessings and peace be on him. This last guidance confirms and includes, not controverts and excludes, all previous guidance.

> All mankind were one single community; [then they began to differ] so God sent forth the Prophets as heralds of glad tidings and as warners, and He sent down with them the Book with the truth, that it might decide between the people with regard to all in which they differed (al-Baqarah 2: 213).

> God – there is no god but He, the Ever-living, the Self-subsisting [by whom all subsist]; He has sent down upon you the Book with the truth, confirming what came before it, and He sent down the Torah and the Gospel aforetime, all as guidance unto mankind; and

14

it is He who has sent down the Criterion [by which to discern the true from the false] (Āl 'Imrān 3: 2–4).

And what We have revealed to you in the Book, that is the truth, confirming what came before it; surely God is aware of and sees His servants (al-Fāṭir 35: 31).

With the truth We have sent it down, and with the truth it has come down; and We have sent you but as a herald of glad tidings and a world (al-Isrā' 17: 105).

These are the verses of the Book; and that which has been sent down to you from your Lord is the truth, but most people do not believe (al-Ra'd 13: 1).

Thus, the very simple truths to which Muslims witness – that there is no god but the One God and that Muhammad is God's Messenger – do in fact encompass the whole Truth, all that is true and right and real, all knowledge that is trustworthy. The Shahadah to God is the proclamation of, and commitment to, His lordship over everything in the heavens and on earth; more specifically, over all human life. Shahadah to Muhammad, blessings and peace be on him, is no parochial call to an exclusive or tribal faith and way of life, for he confirms and enfolds every Truth before him. Witness to him, therefore, is witness to every Messenger of God, to the profound reality of the continuing act of Divine guidance.

Witnessing, according to the Qur'ān, is indeed a Divine act: God Himself witnesses to the Truth, so do His Angels, and all those who possess knowledge. Thus, in witnessing to the Truth, the Muslim in fact becomes a party to the Divine testimony. And, on the Day of Judgement, man's ears, eyes, hands, feet, and body, too, will become witnesses as to how truthful was his witness during his life on earth.

God bears witness that there is no god but He – and the Angels, and all those possessing knowledge – upholding justice, there is no god but He, the All-mighty, the All-wise (Āl 'Imrān 3: 18).

15

But, God [Himself] bears witness to [the truth of] what He has sent down to you; He has sent down that with His knowledge, and the Angels also bear witness; and God is sufficient as a witness (al-Nisā' 4: 166).

Say: What could most weightily bear witness [to the Truth]? Say: God is witness between me and you, and this Qur'ān has been revealed to me so that I may warn you thereby, and whomsoever it may reach. Do you indeed bear witness that there are other gods with God? Say: I bear no [such] witness. Say: He is the One God; and I am quit of what you associate (al-An'ām 6: 19).

Till, when they come to it [the Fire], their hearing, and their sights, and their skins will bear witness against them, speaking of what they were doing. And they will say to their skins: Why did you bear witness against us? They shall say: God has given speech to us, as He gives speech to everything (Fuṣṣilat 41: 20–1).

The Inherent Logic of Truth

Truth, of whatever nature and form and wherever it is, by the compulsive logic inherent in its nature, requires to be manifest, to be known. That is the primary reason why God witnesses to the truth about Him, to the truth of His guidance. That is why everything that He has created, too, manifests not only its own true nature but also witnesses to God, and witnesses to every truth. It is only a creation possessing free will, such as man, who may conceal the truth of its own nature, the truth it may possess, or the truth about its Creator.

The seven heavens extol His limitless glory, and the earth, and whatever is in them; and there is not a single thing but which glorifies Him with His praise, but you do not understand their glorification. Surely He is All-forbearing, All-forgiving (al-Isrā' 17: 44).

16

Have you not seen that before God prostrate themselves
all that are in the heavens and all that are on earth –
the sun, and the moon, and the stars, and the mountains,
and the trees, and the beasts? And many of mankind;
but many [others, having denied Him] will merit punishment (al-Ḥajj 22: 18).

Thus, those who have been given the Truth, too, are under
pledge – by the logic of truth itself, by the logic of having
Divine guidance, and by the logic of their human nature, of
their particular history, of their explicit and implicit covenant
with God – to bear witness to it, to make it manifest. This
argument runs like a thread through all the Quranic dis-
courses which urge upon man, in general, and upon certain
groups and communities, in particular, to fulfil their pledge,
by reminding them of His bounties and favours, of their
history, and of the fact of having been given His guidance.

And when God made covenant with those who had
been given the Book: you shall make it known to
mankind, and not conceal it (Āl 'Imrān 3: 187).

Children of Israel, remember My blessing with which I
blessed you, and fulfil [your] covenant with Me and I
shall fulfil [My] covenant with you (al-Baqarah 2: 40;
also 5: 12 and 7: 169).

[Believers], remember God's blessing upon you, and
your covenant [with Him] which He made with you,
when you said: We have heard, and we obey (al-Mā'idah
5: 7).

Those who conceal the clear messages and the guidance
that We have sent down, after We have made them
clear for mankind in the Book – they shall be cursed
by God and the cursers; except such as repent, and put
themselves right, and make [the Book] known . . .
(al-Baqarah 2: 159–60).

This last passage clearly states that the whole rationale for the duty of witness is inherent in the fact of having the Book: it has been given by God, it is a clear guidance, it has been given and made clear *for* mankind. Therefore, those who possess the Book must make it clear before mankind. Otherwise, they deserve to be cursed by God and all those who are deprived of the guidance, unless they repent and present its message clearly.

Human Destiny and the Witness

This witness to the Truth is most critical for human destiny. Truth must be manifest and known, not only because of its inherent logic, but more importantly because human beings can neither fulfil the meaning and purpose in their lives nor can they achieve the glory that is their destiny without receiving the Truth. The Quranic discourse in this regard is very important and should be clearly understood.

Firstly, that man has been given life to test how he conducts himself in fulfilling the purpose of his creation during his sojourn on earth. Secondly, that he has been created to live in surrender to his Creator. Thirdly, that he will be judged for his *whole* life, and for *all* of its consequences, even beyond life, after his earthly life comes to an end. Then he will be either rewarded or punished in accordance with his conduct. Fourthly, that his real destiny lies in the life that will follow this judgement, the *Ākhirah*. Hence he must be judged fairly and mercifully. Fifthly, that he must therefore be made aware of what his Creator desires of him, how he must conduct himself. Sixthly, that to meet this urgent need of man, God has always sent His Messengers to guide man; indeed, the very first man, Adam, was a Messenger.*

---

* See note 1 on p. 49 for a more detailed discussion of the Quranic discourse on this issue.

18

This, then, is the Divine law under which man's ultimate destiny critically hinges on the successful rendering of the witness to the Truth.

The Responsibility of the Ummah

Once the Quranic discourse in this respect is fully understood, it should not be difficult to see how the Muslim Ummah as the successor to the Last Prophet, blessings and peace be on him, now bears the responsibility of witness before all mankind for all times to come.

Firstly, all the Messengers of God discharged this duty during their lifetime, the last of them being the Prophet Muhammad, blessings and peace be on him. The Qur'ān addresses him thus, defining all the duties entrusted to him:

> O Prophet, We have sent you as a witness [to the Truth], and as a herald of glad tidings and a warner, and as one who calls to God, by His leave, and as a light-giving lamp (al-Aḥzāb 33: 45–6).

Secondly, the Prophet, blessings and peace be on him, was the Messenger to all mankind, and not merely to the Arabs, and for all times to come, by virtue of being the Last Prophet.

> We have not sent you [O Prophet] but to the entire mankind, to be a herald of glad tidings and a warner; however most people do not understand (Sabā' 34: 28).

> Say [O Prophet]: O mankind, surely I am the Messenger of God to all of you, of Him to whom belongs the kingdom of the heavens and of the earth. There is no god but He. He gives life, and makes to die. Believe then in God, and in His Messenger, the unlettered Prophet, who believes in God and His words, and follow him, so that you might find guidance (al-A'rāf 7: 158).

> Muhammad is not the father of anyone of your men,

but the Messenger of God, and the Seal of all Prophets;
God has knowledge of everything (al-Aḥzāb 33: 40).

Thirdly, though the Prophet has died, the Book that he
was given by God and that he delivered, the Qur'ān,
continues to live exactly as he delivered it. On this point
there is no disagreement, even by those who do not believe
in his prophethood. This is a result of God's promise.

> Indeed, it is We who have sent down the reminder;
> and, indeed, it is We who shall truly guard it (al-Ḥijr
> 15: 9).

Fourthly, the need to witness God's guidance before
mankind remains as necessary and as urgent as ever. Therefore, being in possession of the last Book of God, free from
any corruption, the Muslims stand charged with fulfilling this
need. Their duty to witness is a corollary to the Prophet's
duty to witness, as the Qur'ān explains. That is why the duty
of Jihad has been enjoined upon them, and has been made
the measure and criterion of true Iman. Jihad does not
amount only to waging war, but is primarily intended to
discharge this duty of witness. Moreover, it has been made
clear in the Qur'ān that this Ummah does not exist for its
own self-interest or its own self-salvation, but that it has
been brought into existence for the good of all mankind.

> O believers, bow down and prostrate yourselves, and
> serve only your Lord, and do good, so that you might
> attain well-being. And struggle in the way of God as
> ought to be struggled in His way. He has chosen you,
> and He has not laid on you in your Din any constriction.
> Follow the way of your father, Abraham. He has named
> you Muslims, before and in this, so that the Messenger
> would be a witness before you, and you would be
> witnesses before all mankind. So establish the Prayer,
> give the Alms, and hold fast unto God. He is your
> Master. How excellent the Master, and how excellent
> the Helper (al-Ḥajj 22: 77–8).

Believers are those who [truly] believe in God and His
Messenger, then hesitate not, and who strive hard with
their possessions and their selves in the way of God; it
is they who are the truthful ones (al-Ḥujurāt 49: 15).

You are the best community brought forth for mankind:
you enjoin the right and forbid the wrong, and you
believe in God (Āl 'Imrān 3: 110).

It is important to remember that this duty has been laid
down upon the whole Ummah, and is obligatory on every
one of its members. But it is so important that, if every
member of the Ummah does not perform this duty, it has
been laid down that there must at least be one group among
them who should take upon itself this task.

There must be one group among you, who invites to
good, and enjoins the right and forbids the wrong (Āl
'Imrān 3: 104).

Sayyid Mawdudi's Call

The above reflections have been made with the intention
of putting Sayyid Mawdudi's discourse in its proper Quranic
perspective. These, along with the notes appended to his
text, should, *inshā'allāh*, help to illuminate his message with
the light of the Qur'ān. For, he does no more than renew
and repeat the call made by the Qur'ān upon Allah's
Messenger and the Muslim Ummah from the very beginning.
The first message that came from God called upon the
Prophet, and therefore his Ummah, to 'read' (*iqra*). The
message that immediately followed – 'arise and warn' (*qum
fa andhir*) – determined for ever that having and reading the
Book must result in calling all mankind to their Creator and
warning them of the consequences of rebelling against Him.
The Prophet's, blessings and peace be on him, last public

act was to make his audience witness that he had fulfilled his own duty of witness to them.

Since this address was delivered, about four decades ago, the state of the Muslim Ummah has worsened. Although country after country has gained independence, at least in appearance, they have gained no honour, dignity and respect. The Muslim societies remain as indifferent to their duty as ever. Instead, they are dedicated to the pursuit of the same ideals as are non-Muslims. Modernization and economic progress are the goals on which all their efforts and energies are concentrated. These have become the new gods whom they worship. The results are there for all to see. They remain ridden by bitter internal strifes and divisions, poverty and backwardness. Muslim states, from one end to the other, are plagued by autocratic and despotic regimes which suppress the Muslim masses and their aspirations, deny them even fundamental human rights, even a share in governing themselves. Muslim blood still flows like water. Large Muslim minorities, as in the USSR, India, China, and Israel, still live as second-class citizens, constantly in fear of life and honour. In short, the Muslim Ummah remains afflicted by degradation and humiliation, ignominy and powerlessness.

At the same time, all the 'cures' applied by modernist, secularist and Westernized elites have miserably failed to improve their lot. Simply because, as Sayyid Mawdudi says, their condition will never change unless they begin to fulfil the covenant that God has made with them. The only redeeming feature, perhaps, is that during the last fifty years, as a result of the work done by such persons as Sayyid Mawdudi, many strong Islamic movements have sprung up, and a very large number of Muslims, especially the youth, are dedicating themselves to the mission of being witnesses unto mankind.

It is therefore time that we listen with greater attention to the call of the Qur'ān which Sayyid Mawdudi has so eloquently and passionately presented to us in this address:

When a people turn away from God's guidance, when they are guilty of perjury and disloyalty to their Creator, when they turn traitors to him, then God punishes them severely in this world.

If you are being trampled upon today, if you fear greater catastrophes tomorrow, is this not but the punishment for your false witness and concealment of the Truth?

To my mind, your destiny, now and ever, depends on one issue only: how you conduct yourselves in respect of God's guidance that has come to you through His Messenger, blessings and peace be on him.

This [glorious] future is yours! But only if you follow Islam sincerely and exclusively and serve as its faithful witnesses.

1

Witness to the Truth

Praise and Salutations

All praise be to God who alone is the Creator, Master and Sovereign of the universe. It is He who rules over it with perfect wisdom, absolute power and infinite mercy. He who has created man, endowed him with knowledge and reason, made him His vicegerent on earth, and has sent His Books and Messengers to guide him.

May God bless all those righteous and noble servants of His who were appointed to teach man how to live as true human beings and who made man aware of the real purpose of his life, and showed him the right way to live in this world. Whatever measure of true guidance, morality, piety, and selflessness that the world possesses today, it owes to the teachings of these servants of God, peace be upon them. This is a debt that can never be sufficiently repaid.

Our Message

Brothers and friends, we usually divide our meetings into two parts. In one part, we review, among ourselves, our activities and discuss plans for their advancement. The other part we devote to conveying our message to the people of the area where we hold our meeting. We have, thus, asked you to join us in this meeting so that we may explain our message to you.

This address was delivered at a conference of Jama'at Islami, Lahore Division, held at Muradpur, Sialkot, then in pre-partition India, on 30 December, 1946.

On the one hand our message is addressed to Muslims, and on the other hand to all those human beings who are outside the fold of Islam. It is unfortunate, however, that I do not see here today people belonging to the second category. Our past mistakes and present errors are responsible for alienating a great many people from us. Therefore, we hardly ever find the opportunity either to draw them near to us or draw near to them, so that we may communicate to them the message sent by God, in whom we all believe, through His Messengers for the guidance of us all. Since we do not have any non-Muslims present amongst us, I shall only concentrate upon that part of our message which is meant for Muslims.

The Purpose and Duty of the Muslim Ummah

Responsibilities and Duties

To the Muslims we have only one very simple thing to say: Understand and fulfil the responsibilities and duties that fall upon you by virtue of your being Muslims. You cannot get away with merely affirming that you are Muslims and that you have accepted God as your only God and Islam as your religion. Rather, as soon as you acknowledge Allah as your only Lord and His guidance as your way of life, you take upon yourselves certain obligations and duties. These obligations you must always remain conscious of, these duties you must always endeavour to discharge. If you evade them, you shall not escape the evil consequences of your conduct in this world or in the Hereafter.

What are these duties? They are not merely confined to the affirmation of faith in Allah, His Angels, His Books, His Messengers, and the Day of Judgement. Nor are they confined to performing the Prayers, observing the Fasts, going on the Pilgrimage, and paying the Alms. Nor are these duties exhausted by observing the injunctions of Islam relating to marriage, divorce and inheritance. Over and above all these duties, there is one which is the most important: that your lives bear witness to the Truth that you have been given by God before all mankind, the Truth which you believe to be true.

The Only Purpose of Existence

The Qur'ān clearly states that witnessing to the Truth in a manner that would leave mankind with no justifiable ground to deny it is the only purpose behind constituting you as a distinct Ummah (community), named Muslims.

> And thus We have made you a community of the middle way, so that you may be witnesses [to the Truth] before all mankind, and the Messenger may be witness [to it] before you (al-Baqarah 2: 143).

This mission is the sole objective for which your Ummah has been brought into being, it is the *raison d'être* of its existence as a society of human beings. Unless you fulfil it you are squandering your life. For this is no ordinary duty; it is a duty enjoined on you by God. It is a Divine command and a Divine call:

> O believers, be ever steadfast in standing up, for the sake of God, bearing witness to justice (al-Mā'idah 5: 8).

It is not a mere trifle but an emphatic and grave mandate, for Allah also says:

> And who is a greater wrong-doer than he who suppresses a witness entrusted to him by God (al-Baqarah 2: 140).

You have been warned of the consequences of evading this duty. Look at the history of the people of Israel. They

too were appointed to stand in the witness-box; but sometimes they suppressed the Truth, and sometimes they witnessed against it. By their conduct, they, in fact, became
witnesses to falsehood rather than witnesses to the Truth.
The consequence was that God forsook them and a curse
fell upon them.

> And so, humiliation and powerlessness afflicted them,
> and they earned God's anger (al-Baqarah 2: 61).

Witness to the Truth

What does this duty of witness imply? Consider it carefully:
You have been given Divine guidance, you have been shown
the Truth. You must, therefore, establish by your testimony
and witness its authenticity and truthfulness before all
mankind. This is a testimony that will make the authenticity
and truthfulness of Divine guidance self-evident, for all to
see, and a witness that will make it clear and indisputable
for all people.

For this very purpose all the Messengers were sent to the
world; this was their primary duty. After them, their followers were entrusted with the same duty. And now the Muslim
Ummah, as the successor to the Last Prophet, blessings and
peace be on him, is charged with this very mission, just as
he was charged with it during his lifetime.

Nature and Importance

What is the importance of this witness? You will know its
importance only when you understand that man has been
made accountable for his conduct and will be rewarded and
punished in the Hereafter under the Divine Law which rests
entirely on this witness. God is All-wise, All-merciful, and
All-just. His mercy, justice and wisdom are not such that He
should punish people for living against His will while they
had no knowledge of it, that He should take people to task

28

for deviating from the right path of which they were ignorant, that He should hold people accountable for things of which they were unaware.[1]

It was as a provision against this that the first man He created was a Messenger, and that after him many more were sent from time to time.[2] They were all to be witnesses to mankind, to make it understand and remember the will of God. They were all to teach human beings the proper way of conducting their lives, the code of behaviour that they should adopt to win God's favour, the acts that they should perform, the acts that they should avoid, and the things for which they will be brought to account.[3]

This witness was given by Allah's Messengers so that the people may not be in a position to say to God: How can we be punished for things of which we were not warned? The Qur'ān says:

> [We sent] all Messengers as heralds of glad tidings and as warners, so that men may not have any argument against God, after [the coming of] these Messengers; God is indeed All-mighty, All-wise (al-Nisā' 4: 165).

In this manner God made His Messengers bear the crucial responsibility for guiding man on His behalf. They were thus charged with a very delicate and grave responsibility: if they bore witness to the Truth properly, the people would be accountable for their own actions, but if they failed in their duty, they themselves would be called to account for their people going astray. In other words, unless the Messengers made people responsible for their conduct by giving them conclusive and indisputable testimony to the Truth, the people would hold the Messengers responsible for their own misdeeds, saying: 'The knowledge that God gave you, that you did not communicate to us; the way of life that He showed you, that you did not show us.'[4] That is why all the Messengers always remained acutely conscious of the burden of this responsibility, and that is why they endeavoured so hard to bear witness before the people to the Truth entrusted to them.[5]

Responsibility of the Ummah

All those who were led by the Messengers to the knowledge of the Truth and Divine guidance were formed into a community, an Ummah. Every Ummah was charged with the same mission as the Messengers of witnessing to the Truth. As successors to the Messengers, every Ummah has the same crucial role and responsibility as they had. Thus, if an Ummah properly fulfils its duty of witnessing to the Truth and yet the people do not pay heed, it will be rewarded and the people will be brought to account. However, if the Ummah neglects its duty, or if it gives false witness, it will deserve to be punished more severely than the people. The Ummah shall be accountable not only for its own misdeeds, but also for the misdeeds of those who went astray or turned to error and wickedness because the testimony given to them by the Ummah was misleading or false.

This, brothers, is the nature and logic of that grave and crucial duty which lies upon me, you and all those who consider themselves part of the Muslim Ummah, or those who have become sufficiently aware of God's Book and the guidance brought by His Messengers.

How Should We Witness to the Truth?

Let us now see in what manner we should discharge our duty of witnessing to the Truth. Witnessing is of two types: one, witness by words, or the word-witness; the other, witness by acts and deeds, or the act-witness.[6]

Word-witness

In what way should our words witness to the Truth? Through our speech and writing, we should proclaim and explain to the world the guidance that has come to us through God's Messengers. This, in sum, is the word-witness. Employing all possible methods of education, using all possible means of communication and propagation, mastering all knowledge provided by the contemporary arts and sciences, we should inform mankind of the way of life that God has laid down for man. The guidance that Islam gives to humanity in thought and belief, in morality and behaviour, in culture and civilization, in economics and business, in jurisprudence and judiciary, in politics and civil administration – that is, in all aspects of inter-human relations – we should clearly and fully expound before mankind. By rational discourse and convincing evidence, we should establish its truth and soundness. By soundly reasoned critique, we should rebut all that is contrary to the guidance given by God.

The task is enormous. Full justice cannot be done to it unless the thought of guiding man to the right path seizes the whole Ummah as completely as it did each Messenger personally. It is essential, too, that this task should become the central objective of all our collective endeavours, that we should commit all our hearts and minds, all of our resources, to this cause. Uppermost in all our actions should be this objective. Under no circumstances should we allow any voice within ourselves to bear witness against the Truth and Divine guidance that we have.

Act-witness

In what way should our acts and deeds witness to the Truth? For this purpose, the guidance that we hold to be true we must put into practice. Our actions should demonstrate the principles we profess to believe in.

Put simply: let our lives speak the truth, and let the world hear it not merely from our lips but also from our deeds; let mankind witness all the blessings that the Divine guidance brings to human life. Let the world taste in our conduct, individual and collective, that sweetness and flavour which only the faith in One God can impart to character and morality. Let the world see what fine examples of humanity are fashioned by Islam, what a just society is established, what a sound social order emerges, what a clean and noble civilization arises, how science, literature, and art flourish and develop on sound lines, what a just economy – compassionate and free from conflict – is brought about. Indeed, how every aspect of life is set right, developed and enriched.

We shall not be doing our duty to this task unless our lives, individual and collective, become a living embodiment of Islam: unless our personal characters are a living proof of its truth, our homes are fragrant with its teachings, our businesses and factories are illuminated by its rules and laws, our schools and institutions are shaped by its ideas and norms, and our literature and media reflect its principles. Indeed until our entire national policy and public life make its truth manifest and self-evident.

In short, wherever and whenever any individual or people come in contact with us it is our duty to convince them, by our example, that the principles and teachings which Islam proclaims to be true are indeed true, and that they do improve the quality of human life and raise it to better and higher levels.

The Islamic State

Finally, I should state one more important thing. This witness of ours would not be complete unless we establish a state based on the principles and teachings of Islam. By translating its ideals and practices, its norms and values, its rules and laws, into public policies and programmes, such a state would demonstrate how the Divine guidance leads to equity and justice, reform and upliftment, caring and efficient administration, social welfare, peace and order, high standards of morality in public servants, virtue and righteousness in internal policies, honesty in foreign policies, civilized conduct in war, integrity and loyalty in peace. Such public conduct would be a living testimony for all mankind that Islam is indeed the true guarantor of human well-being, that only following its tenets can ensure the good of mankind.

Only when the Truth is witnessed in this manner, by both words and actions, will the crucial responsibility laid upon the Muslim Ummah be fully discharged. Only then will no ground remain for mankind to deny or turn away from the Divine guidance. Only then, in the Hereafter, will the Muslim Ummah be in a position to take the witness-stand after the Prophet, blessings and peace be on him, and declare that: Whatever truth and guidance we were given by this Prophet, that we conveyed to mankind; those who did not follow it are themselves to blame for going astray, not us.

This is the real meaning and scope of the witness that we as Muslims *ought* to have been giving to the world, both by our words and our deeds. But now let us turn to the actual state of affairs and examine the witness that we in fact *are* giving in favour of the Divine guidance.

Where Do We Stand?

Our Word-witness

First, look at the testimony that is being given by our word-witness. There are few people amongst us who are using their tongues and pens to witness to the truth of Islam. Still fewer in number are those who are doing so in an appropriate and adequate manner. Otherwise, in almost every respect Muslims, on the whole, are giving their witness against Islam and not in its favour as they should.

What is the witness of our landlords? That the Islamic law

of inheritance is wrong and that the customs which came down from the pre-Islamic days are correct. What is the witness of our lawyers and judges? That all the laws of Islam are bad laws, and that their very basis – the sovereignty of God – is unacceptable. They tell us that only the man-made laws, which have come to us through the British, are good laws.

What is the witness of our teachers and educational institutions? That in philosophy and science, history and sociology, economics and politics, law and ethics, the only true and valid knowledge and thought is that derived from the Western secular world-view. That in all these disciplines the Islamic approach is not even worthy of consideration. What is the witness of our writers? That their literature has the same message to impart as that of the godless writers of the secular West. They demonstrate that as Muslims they have no distinctive literary approach of their own. What is the witness of our press and media? That the only issues and debates that they consider important and which preoccupy them, and the only methods and standards of communication that they consider fit to employ, are those which bear the hallmark of the non-Muslim media.

What is the witness of our businessmen and industrialists? That the rules laid down by Islam for economic transactions are impracticable, that business can be conducted only by the methods devised by Kafirs.* What is the witness of our leaders and rulers? That they have the same slogans of nationalism and motherland to mobilize people, the same goals to pursue on national levels, the same methods of solving national problems, the same principles of politics and constitution-making, as are practised by Kafirs. They declare that Islam has no guidance to offer in this respect.

And what is the witness of our masses? They testify that they have nothing to speak about except worldly matters, that they have no such Din which desires to be propagated

---

* Kafir, and Kufr, denote a variety of attitudes and conduct towards the Truth: unbelief, disbelief, denial, rejection, or hostility.

or which demands that they spend part of their time for this purpose. This, then, is the state of witness being given by our whole Ummah by means of its words. This is the case not only in this country but throughout the whole world.

Our Act-witness

Now let us turn to our act-witness and look at the witness being given by our actions and deeds. Here our conduct is even more scandalous than that in respect of our witness by words. No doubt there are a few good Muslims whose lives are a true example of Islam. But consider how the over-whelming majority of the Ummah, the society at large, is conducting itself.

What is the witness being given by the life of a typical, ordinary Muslim? That the persons shaped and moulded by Islam are in no way better than, or different from, those prepared by Kufr. If anything, the former are worse than the latter: for instance, it is more likely that a Muslim would speak a lie, that he would betray and breach a trust placed in him, that he would oppress people and do wrong to them, that he would abandon his promise, that he would steal and rob, that he would engage himself in disorderly and violent conduct, that he would indulge in all sorts of indecent acts. Indeed, in respect of all these immoral actions the level of Muslim 'performance' is no less than that of any Kafir people.

What is the witness of our social life? Look at our life-styles, our customs and ceremonies, our festivities, our fairs and religious gatherings, our meetings and processions: in no aspect do we truly represent Islam. Indeed, on the contrary, our social life is a pathetic testimony that the followers of Islam consider the un-Islamic ways to be better and preferable than the Islamic.

Similar is the testimony of our other social institutions and collective pursuits. When we set up educational institutions, we import everything from Kafirs – our knowledge, our educational system, our philosophy, our spirit and objective.

When we form parties and associations, we model everything on the patterns set by Kafirs – our ideals and goals, our structures and constitutions, our policies and methods. When we, as a people, launch a struggle, our cause, our slogans and demands, our issues and debates, our programmes and procedures, our resolutions, statements, and speeches, are all true replicas of the practices of Kafir communities and nations.

Things have come to such a pass that even our independent states, where they exist, have borrowed their constitutions, their codes of law, and their guiding policies and principles from Kafirs. In some states, the Islamic law has been reduced to a mere personal law; in some others even this personal law has been altered. An English writer tauntingly remarks:

> In view of the many charges levelled by Indians at the British administration, it is important to realize that the British were extraordinarily slow to introduce any innovations in the law . . . [Indeed] as far as Islam is concerned the result of the British connexion with India has been to establish on a firmer basis the Muslim personal and religious law . . . while all the rest of the *shari‘a* has been abolished . . .
>
> On the other hand Albania and Turkey have both become secular states [adopting European penal and civil codes, even altering Muslim penal law] . . . [Thus, it can be said, as Lindsay says, that] 'The Muslim doctrine that legislation is not within the competence of an earthly sovereign was never, indeed, anything more than a pious fiction . . .'*

This, then, is the witness being given by the actions of almost all Muslims. This witness, too, goes against Islam. It is not in its favour. Whatever lip-service we might pay to Islam, our public conduct proves that there is no aspect of Islam that we approve of, that we do not consider its laws to be good and conducive to our well-being.

---

* Laurence Browne, *The Prospects of Islam,* (London, 1944), pp. 31–5.

And With What Consequences!

Our Punishment

In view of our conduct, we are guilty of giving false witness, of perjury and concealing the Truth. As a consequence, we are facing precisely the same punishment that has been prescribed in the Law of God for such grave and heinous crimes.

What is this law? When a people reject and turn away from God's guidance, when they are guilty of perjury and disloyalty to their Creator, and when they turn traitors to Him, then God punishes them severely in this world as well as in the world-to-come.[7] This law was applied to the Children of Israel.[8] Now it is we, the Muslim Ummah, who stand in the dock. God had no personal vendetta against the Jews that He should have punished only them. Nor does He have any kinship or special relationship with Muslims that He should set us free even though we are now committing the same crime as they did then.[9]

In This World

The punishment meted out to Muslims for their crimes in this world is there for all to see. Indeed, the extent and pace of our decline has been in true proportion to the extent and pace of our negligence and failure to do our duty to witness to the Truth and our 'progress' in witnessing to falsehood. During the last one hundred years, from Morocco to Indonesia, country after country has been lost by us to alien subjugation; one Muslim people after another have fallen under the yoke of colonial rule and domination. No longer does the word 'Muslim' stand for dignity, no longer does it command respect; rather it has become a mark of degradation, humiliation, gross backwardness, and utter powerlessness.

How powerless have we become? We have lost all honour

and respect in the eyes of the world. In some places, our blood has flowed like water and we have been subjected to large-scale massacres; in other places, we have been driven out of our homes; in others, we have been tortured and persecuted; in still others, we have been reduced to living as serfs. If in some places Muslim states have survived, they have suffered defeat after defeat until they have been reduced to positions of fear and impotency in the face of foreign powers. If only they had witnessed to Islam by their words and deeds, the secular powers would have stood in awe of them.

Why go so far afield? Just look at your situation in India.* Because you evaded your duty of bearing witness to the truth of Islam, indeed because you went further and gave false witness against it both by your words and deeds, the entire country was wrested from your control. First, you were vanquished by the Marathas and Sikhs, and later, servitude to the British rule became your fate. And now still greater calamities stare you in the face.

Today your minority status has become your greatest anxiety; you live in fear of the Hindu majority lest it subjugates you and you meet the same fate as did the untouchables. But, for God's sake, tell me: Could a majority have threatened you if you had only been true witnesses of Islam? Will not this problem of majority and minority vanish within a few years if today your words and actions bear true witnesses to Islam?

In Arabia, an extremely hostile and oppressive majority set out to exterminate an insignificant minority of about one in one hundred thousand. With what result? Within ten years, this minority, by its truthful and trustworthy witness in favour of Islam, turned into a one hundred per cent majority. Later, when these witnesses of Islam emerged from Arabia, within twenty-five years, from Turkistan to Morocco, people after people trusted the probity of their

---

* This address was delivered before India was partitioned and Pakistan was established on 14 August, 1947.

38

witness and joined them in their faith. Where no one but Zoroastrians, Christians and pagans once lived, now only Muslims live. No intransigence, no chauvinism, no religious bigotry, proved strong enough to resist the living, true witness of the Divine guidance that Muslims gave.

If you are being trampled upon today, if you fear greater catastrophes tomorrow, is this not but the punishment for your false witness and concealment of the Truth?

Punishment in the World-to-Come

This is the punishment you are receiving in this world; but a more severe punishment is likely to be meted out to you in the world-to-come. How can you be absolved of the blame for every evil and every wrong to which man has been subjected only because you failed to do your duty as witnesses of the Truth? Unless you do your duty, whatever oppression and corruption is perpetrated in the world and whatever immorality and wickedness prevails, there is no reason why you should not be held accountable for it. You may not be responsible for originating them yourselves, but you are certainly responsible, because of your false witness, for maintaining and perpetuating them, for their origination by others, and for allowing them to spread.

What is Our Real Problem?

Pseudo Problems

By now, brothers, you must have understood how we, as Muslims, *ought* to have been living and behaving, and how we in fact *are* living and behaving. You must also have realized what grave consequences we are suffering because of our conduct. You should, therefore, have no difficulty in seeing that the problems which Muslims consider crucial for their societies and which they are doing their utmost to solve by various devices – some of them invented by them, but mostly copied from others – are *not* their real problem. The time, energy and resources that they spend on solving these problems are simply being wasted.

For example, we look upon ourselves as a minority engulfed by an overwhelming alien majority, or as a majority deprived of its sovereignty within its own territory, or as a nation subjugated and exploited by a foreign power, or as a people suffering from backwardness and poverty. Then we devote all our efforts to achieving objectives which emanate from these conceptions and images of ourselves. For instance, to objectives such as safeguarding and securing our status in a country as a minority, or to achieving sovereignty within our territorial boundaries, or to winning freedom from foreign domination, or to achieving the same levels of economic progress and development as those of the advanced nations.

These and other similar issues may be the foremost concerns of those who are not Muslims, who do not accept God as their Lord and Guide, and may form the central objects of their endeavours. But for us Muslims they are not the primary problems; we face them only because we have been, and still are, neglecting to do our duty. Had we been true witnesses of Islam, we would not have found ourselves lost in such a dense jungle of complex and inextricable problems. If we now direct all our attention and endeavours to doing our duty instead of dissipating our energies on clearing the woods, they will clear in no time, and not only for ourselves but for all mankind. For, keeping the world clean and improving it is our responsibility; as we have forsaken our appointed duty, the world has become infested with thorny woods. And no wonder that the most thorny part has fallen to our lot.

Unfortunately, our religious and political leaders do not try to understand this simple but crucial reality. Everywhere they continue to convince the Muslims that their problems are the problems of a minority as against a majority, of material progress, of national security, of winning freedom and independence as a nation state. Furthermore, even the solutions that they recommend have been borrowed from non-Muslims. But just as I believe in God, so I believe that you are being misled, and that by following such paths you will never achieve your well-being and destiny.

Our Real Problem

What, then, is our real problem? If I do not tell you that clearly, without any reservation, I shall be doing you a great disservice. To my mind, your destiny, now and ever, depends on one issue only: How do you conduct yourselves in respect of God's guidance that has come to you through His Messenger, blessings and peace be on him?

Because of this guidance you are Muslims. Because of this guidance, whether you like it or not, you have agreed to become ambassadors of Islam to the entire world. Therefore, only if you follow Islam totally and devotedly, if your words and actions bear true witness to its teachings, if your social and public conduct faithfully represents every aspect of Islam, will you rise from glory to glory in this world, and receive highest honours in the world-to-come. Then, in no time, the dark clouds of fear and anxiety, of disgrace and humiliation, of subjugation and slavery will disperse. Then, the truth of your message and the virtue of your character will capture mind after mind and heart after heart. Then, your prestige and reputation, your influence and authority, will hold sway over the world. Hopes of securing justice will be pinned on you, trust will be placed in your integrity and honesty, prospects of virtue will be confided in you, and authority will be accorded to your world.

In contrast, the leaders of secularism will lose all credibility and authority. Their philosophy and world-view, their economic and political ideologies, will prove fake and spurious when confronted by your truth and right conduct.

The forces that today belong to the secular camp will, one by one, break away and join the camp of Islam. A time will, then, come when communism will live in fear of its very survival in Moscow itself, when capitalist democracy will shudder at the thought of defending itself even in Washington and New York, when materialist secularism will be unable to find a place even in the universities of London and Paris, when racialism and nationalism will not win even one devotee even among the Brahmans and Germans.

The present era of abject humiliation will, then, become consigned to the pages of history. It will only serve to remind us of the days when the followers of a faith as universal and powerful as Islam were reduced to such stupidity that they trembled in the face of sticks and ropes while they held the staff of Moses under their arm.

This future is yours! But only if you follow Islam sincerely and exclusively and serve as its faithful witnesses. Your present conduct, however, is entirely contrary. You have been blessed with the Divine guidance, but, like a snake guarding treasure, you neither benefit from it yourselves nor allow others to benefit from it. By calling yourselves Muslims, you have assumed for yourselves the position of Islam's representatives, but the combined witness of your words and deeds is being given mostly in favour of Ignorance (*Jāhilīyah*), idolatry, materialism, and immorality. You have the Book of God with you, but you have put it on the shelf and, to seek guidance, you turn to all sorts of persons who lead to Kufr, and to sources which lead you astray. You claim to be the servants of the One God, but in fact you are serving every false god, every Satan, and every power in rebellion against God. You have friends and enemies, but it is always your personal, selfish interests that determine your friendship and enmity. In both cases you use Islam as a party to your cause.

Thus, your conduct has, on the one hand, deprived your lives of the blessings that Islam has to offer you, and, on the other, you are alienating mankind rather than attracting it to Islam. If you continue to behave in this manner, you can attain no good, either in this world or in the world-to-come. Its outcome, according to the Law of God, is that miserable situation in which you find yourselves. What the future holds for you may be much worse.

To be truthful, perhaps, if you remove the label of Islam from yourselves and follow Kufr openly and sincerely, then you might at least make as much worldly progress as America, Russia and Britain have made. But, claiming to be Muslims and yet behaving as non-Muslims, closing the door of Divine guidance to mankind by representing Islam falsely before it, is such a heinous crime that it will never allow you to prosper in this world. There is no way you can avert the punishment prescribed by the Qur'ān for this crime. Jewish history provides a living proof of this reality. You may turn to secular nationalism as a lesser evil, you may get yourself accepted as a separate nation and achieve whatever Muslim nationalism seeks to achieve. But none of this will help you.

There is only one way to ward off the punishment of God. Turn back from your sin, and repent.

2

Jama'at Islami

Our Objective

Now, let me explain what Jama'at Islami stands for. We call upon all those who accept Islam as their Din* to transform their lives into living models of this Din. Every Muslim, as an individual, should establish Islam in his personal life. Every Muslim people, as a society, should implement Islam in their collective lives. We say to them: In your homes and family lives, in your education, literature, and journalism, in your businesses and economic affairs, in your organizations and national institutions, indeed in your entire national policy, you must live by Islam. And, thus, by your words and deeds, you must give truthful witness to Islam before mankind.

We further say to them: The sole objective of your existence, as Muslims, is to establish Islam and bear witness to its truth. On this objective must be centred all your efforts and endeavours. You must give up every word and every work that contradicts this objective, and which gives a false image of Islam. Keeping always in mind this duty to Islam, examine your lives, scrutinize whatever you say and do, and direct all your energies and efforts, spend everything you have, in one pursuit: so that Islam is translated into practice in its fullness, so that true and faithful witness to its teachings is given in every possible manner, so that its message is

---

* Din is a word which means much more than a religion or a way of life. It grasps the totality of human life.

45

conveyed to the world in a way that leaves mankind with no reasonable ground to turn away from it.

Our Method

What is the method which we adopt in pursuit of the above objective, the sole reason for the existence of Jama'at Islami?

ACTIVATING CONSCIOUSNESS. Firstly, we remind Muslims that their foremost duty is to bear witness to Islam before mankind. We make them fully conscious of what Islam is, what it demands of them, what being Muslim means, and, to be true Muslims, what responsibilities they must fulfil.

ESSENTIALITY OF ORGANIZATION. Secondly, once they have fully understood these things and their consciousness has been activated, we say to them: All that Islam requires of you cannot be fulfilled at the individual level, and that organized, collective effort is essential. Only a small part of Islam pertains to individual, private life. Even if you practise that part, Islam will neither be fully realized nor will your duty of witnessing to it be fully discharged. Indeed, if the society is ruled by secularism and Kufr, then it will be impossible to live by Islam even in many aspects of your private life. The domination of the secular structure will squeeze Islam even out of private life and reduce its writ to a narrower and narrower territory.

To establish Islam fully and to witness to it faithfully, it is, therefore, absolutely essential to launch an organized, collective struggle. All those who are conscious of their duties and responsibilities as Muslims, who are determined to discharge them, must unite, must organize themselves, and must make every effort to invite mankind to Islam. They must translate it into practice, remove all those obstacles which hinder and impede the task of calling mankind to Islam (*Da'wah*), and establish it (*iqāmah*).

That is why organized corporate life, that is *jamā'ah*, has been made mandatory in Islam. That is why it is necessary to establish an organized *jamā'ah* before embarking upon Jihad. That is why life without *jamā'ah* has been equated with the life of Ignorance. That is why seceding from *jamā'ah*, it is declared, amounts to seceding from Islam.

This is what the Prophet, blessings and peace be on him, has explained in the following Hadith:

> I give you the five commandments which Allah has given me: (1) *al-jamā'ah*, [that is, join together in organized, corporate life,] (2) *al-sam'*, [that is, hear attentively and prepare willingly to obey,] (3) *al-ṭā'ah*, [that is, obey,] (4) *al-hijrah*, [that is, give up whatever stands in the way of God,] (5) *al-jihād fī sabīli 'l-lāh*, [that is, struggle in the way of God].
> He who secedes from *the* al-Jama'ah as much as a span casts off the bond of Islam from his neck, unless he returns; and he who rallies people to the claims of *Jāhilīyah* (Ignorance) belongs to the people to be thrown into *Jahannam* (Hell).
> The Companions asked: Allah's Messenger, even if he fasts and prays? He replied: Yes, even if he prays and fasts and asserts that he is a Muslim (*Aḥmad, Tirmidhī, Ḥākim,* reported by al-Ḥārith al-Ash'arī).

Three conclusions can be drawn from this Hadith:

Firstly, in order to work for Islam the correct procedure is first to establish an organizational discipline wherein members will hear and obey their leaders, and, then, to take up Hijrah and Jihad, as the situation may warrant.

Secondly, that secession from the al-Jama'ah* is tantamount to secession from Islam. Such secession means that the person concerned is returning to the life of the pre-Islamic days, when the communal life was not organized around obedience to the One God.

Thirdly, that only through corporate life, *jamā'ah*, and

---

* Al-Jama'ah stands for the Muslim Ummah as a whole, or an Islamic state.

collective struggle, Jihad, can we fulfil the main objectives of Islam and most of its requirements. Sayyidina Umar explains the above position beautifully as follows: There is no Islam without *jamā'ah* (*Jāmi' Bayān al-'Ilm* by Ibn 'Abd al-Barr).

JOINING AN ORGANIZATION. We urge all persons who understand our message and become acutely conscious of their responsibility, and who are prepared to sacrifice their ego and self-interest for the sake of Islam, to join organized life and accept its discipline. Before them we place three alternatives, and they are free to follow any of them.

One, join the Jama'at Islami, if you are convinced that our ideal and message, our organization and mode of work, are all fully Islamic; and that our mission is the same mission which the Qur'ān and Hadith lay down for the Muslim Ummah.

Two, you may join some other organization, if, for some reason, you are not satisfied with us and find that other organization working for Islamic ideals on Islamic lines. Had we ourselves come across such an organization, we would most certainly have joined it, for we do not relish the idea of forming a separate organization.

Three, if you are neither satisfied with us nor with any other organization, then you should form a party of your own which is devoted to the ideal of establishing Islam fully and witnessing to it faithfully by words and deeds.

Whichever alternative you follow, we say, you will be on the right path. For, we have not claimed, and cannot do so if we are sane and sensible, that our Jama'at Islami is the only party which is on the right path, and that all those who do not join it are in the wrong. Indeed, we do not call people to our Jama'at; we call them to their duty. All of us are equally responsible to discharge it. As long as you are doing your duty, you are on the right path, whether you work with us or not.

But what we do say to you is that it is totally wrong neither to rise yourselves nor join forces with those who have risen to take up the mission entrusted to the Muslim Ummah. Equally unacceptable is that, on one pretext or another, you evade your duty of establishing Islam and witnessing to its truth. Or, that, instead, you expend your energies on projects that lead to the establishment and maintenance of a Din other than Islam. Or, that your words and deeds witness things other than Islam. You might have got away with your sham excuses and pretexts, if you were dealing with human beings. But you have to reckon with God who is Omniscient and cannot be deceived by any tricks or devices.

MORE THAN ONE ISLAMIC PARTY? Is it right to form many different parties to work for an identical objective? No doubt such a situation appears to be fraught with the danger of division and conflict. But our circumstances are such that there seems to be no alternative. The Islamic Order lies in a state of disarray and disintegration; our task is to rebuild it afresh, not merely to run it. No such al-Jamaʿah exists to which every Muslim is bound to give his allegiance, to secede from which amounts to secession from Islam, to live in isolation from which amounts to living in Ignorance, and which, by its very nature, includes the whole Ummah. Nor can such an al-Jamaʿah be brought into existence from the outset. In the initial stages of the Islamic movement, therefore, it seems inevitable that various organizations, parties, and groups should emerge in their own places, working for the same ideal but following their own methods and plans.

A day will come, we should hope, when all of them will unite. If these groups are free from selfishness, if they avoid taking extreme positions and tendencies, if they work sincerely for the truly Islamic ideal and goal, if they adopt means that are in accord with Islam, there is no reason why they should not unite. Those who march in the cause of Truth cannot remain divided for long; the Truth must ultimately unite them. For, the very nature of the Truth demands unification and cohesion, unity and harmony.

Dissension and sectarianism appear only when falsehood is mingled with the Truth, or the Truth is used as a mask to cover evil.

Duties of Our Members

What do we demand of our members, what duties do we require them to perform? Briefly, we add nothing, not one jot or tittle to the requirements that Islam itself lays down, nor do we subtract anything from these. We place the whole of Islam before every person, and say to him: Accept it knowingly, consciously and freely; fulfil its requirements with understanding and in the right manner; remove from your thoughts, words, and deeds everything and anything that is against the spirit and injunctions of Islam; turn your whole life into a living witness of Islam.

This, then, is the only admission fee for membership of our party; this, then, is the sum total of our membership rules.

Our constitution, our organizational structure, and our message are there for all to see. Let anyone examine them and find for himself that we have neither added to nor subtracted from Islam anything in contravention of the Qur'ān and the Sunnah. Anything adopted by the Jama'at Islami that can be proved to be contradictory to the Qur'ān and the Sunnah, we shall expunge from our party; anything enjoined in the Qur'ān and the Sunnah that can be proved to have been excluded by us, we shall adopt without hesitation. For, we have formed this Jama'at for the purpose of establishing and witnessing to the totality of Islam. Who, then, shall be a greater wrong-doer than us if we prove to be guilty of hypocrisy.

Similarly, the only duty that we ask of those who join us is to witness to Islam by word and example, and to struggle collectively for its translation into practice. By doing so, they will be properly fulfilling their duty of being witnesses unto mankind.

For giving word-witness, we are training our members so

that each one becomes equipped to explain Islam, both by speech and writing, in as reasoned and convincing manner as possible. We are trying to establish institutions, too, which will demonstrate, in a systematic manner and by employing all available means of communication, the truth of Islamic teachings in every branch of human knowledge, and in every problem of human life.

Regarding the word-witness, our efforts are directed, firstly, at transforming every individual into a living example of Islam, and, secondly, developing an organized society consisting of such individuals, wherein the true spirit of Islam will prevail and be manifest. Eventually, this society, through its incessant and utmost striving, should overthrow the domination of Godless systems and replace them with that just system which is a true and faithful example of Islam.

NOTES

by Khurram Murad

1. *Law of God for Judgement*: The Qur'ān has explained in considerable detail the law under which man's accountability on the Day of Judgement depends upon the witness to the Truth rendered by its bearers before him. It is important to understand what the Qur'ān says in this regard.

Firstly, why has man been placed on earth? So that he may use his full and enormous potential to conduct himself in that right manner which will fulfil the meaning in his life.

> And He it is who has created the heavens and the earth in six days, and His throne was upon the waters, so that He might test you which of you is best in conduct (Hūd 11: 7).

> He who has created death and life, so that He might test you, which of you is best in conduct (al-Mulk 67: 2).

> We have made all that is on earth an adornment for it, and so that we might test which of them is best in conduct (al-Kahf 18: 7).

Secondly, what is the meaning and purpose of man's life? That he lives as his Creator desires him to live: in surrender and worship to Him alone. Not because God in any way *needs* his worship, but because man needs to worship only his Creator and none else so that his own nature is not perverted and corrupted, and so that he does not live in opposition to its intrinsic character. Also, only by so living, will his earthly life be set on the right path and will prosper, bringing him peace and happiness (all of which the Qur'ān calls *falāḥ*).

> And I have not created Jinn and mankind except to serve and worship Me. I desire of them no provision, neither do I desire that they should feed Me (al-Dhāriyāt 51: 56–7).

Thirdly, and consequently, man's earthly life must be judged. He must give an account of his conduct, and he must face the consequences of how he lives his life. Obviously, to be judged fairly, this judgement must be made only *after* his earthly life has come to an end, and only *by* the One who gave this life, who knows everything, and who is All-powerful and All-just. Only then can he be judged fairly, and duly rewarded and punished, for everything – from the most hidden innermost thoughts to the consequences of his conduct that extend far and wide, and beyond life for generations to come. The judge, in other words, must be the King and Master of the Day of Judgement.

> What, did you think that We created you in mere idle play, and that you would not be returned to Us? But, high exalted is God, the King, the True! There is no god but He, the Lord of the Noble Throne (al-Mu'minūn 23: 115–16).

> And We have not created the heavens and the earth and all that is between them in mere idle play; We have not created them but with truth [meaning and purpose], but most of them understand it not (al-Dukhān 44: 38–9).

> Or, do those who commit evil deeds think that We shall place them on an equal footing with those who believe and do righteous deeds, both in their life and their death? How bad is their judgement! God has created the heavens and the earth with truth [meaning and purpose], so that every human being shall be recompensed for what he has earned, and they shall not be wronged (al-Jāthiyah 45: 21–2).

> Every human being shall taste death; and you shall surely be paid in full your wages on the Day of Resurrection; whosoever [then] is saved from the Fire and admitted to Paradise, he indeed wins the triumph; worldly life is nothing but enjoyment of delusion (Āl 'Imrān 3: 185).

> And We shall set up just balance-scales on Resurrection Day, and no human being shall be wronged anything; even if it be the weight of a mustard-seed, We shall bring it forth, and sufficient are We as reckoners (al-Anbiyā' 21: 47).

> He knows the [most] stealthy glance, and what the hearts conceal (Ghāfir 40: 19).

Fourthly, therefore, man's ultimate destiny lies in the life to come, in the *Ākhirah*. Equally important is the fact that the account of the *Ākhirah* as given in the Qur'ān clearly demonstrates, and repeatedly emphasizes, that one will be judged there by due process of justice, fairly and equitably, mercifully and kindly. Also, no one will be wronged or dealt with unjustly even by an atom's weight.

> And vie with one another, hastening to forgiveness from your Lord, and to Paradise as vast as the heavens and the earth, which has been prepared for the God-conscious (Āl 'Imrān 3: 133).

> O my people, surely this worldly life is but a brief enjoyment; surely the world to come is the home abiding. [There] whosoever does an evil deed shall be recompensed only with the like of it, but whosoever does righteous deeds – be it man or woman, and is a believer – those shall enter Paradise, therein provided [with blessings] beyond all reckoning (Ghāfir 40: 39–40).

> Surely God shall not wrong so much as an atom's weight (al-Nisā' 4: 40).

Fifthly, in all fairness, therefore, man must be made aware of how he should live his earthly life. In other words, he should know of his Creator and Lord, of what He desires of him, of how He wants him to worship Him and surrender to Him. Unless man knows all this, he cannot be held fully responsible and accountable if he pursues a wrong way of life. Such knowledge has been given to him in his own nature, in the universe around him, and in the revelations sent through God's Messengers.

> And when your Lord brought forth from the Children of Adam, from their loins, their descendants, and made them bear witness about themselves: Am I not your Lord? They said: Yes, we bear witness – lest you say on the Day of Resurrection: We were unaware of this. Or lest you say: Our fathers ascribed partners [to God] aforetime, and we were but their descendants after them. What, wilt Thou then destroy us for the deeds of the vain-doers? (al-A'rāf 7: 172–3).

> How many a sign there is in the heavens and on earth which they pass by [unthinkingly], and on which they turn their backs! And most of them do not believe in God, but they ascribe partners [to Him] (Yūsuf 12: 105–6).

> [And God will say:] O community of jinn and men, did not Messengers come unto you from among you, who conveyed

unto you My revelations and warned you of the meeting of this your day? . . . That is because your Lord would not destroy communities unjustly, while their people are ignorant (al-An'ām 6: 130–1).

Sixthly, for a number of reasons, all of which it is not possible to discuss here, only God, and no one else, can provide man with the knowledge of the right guidance. Firstly and primarily, because only He can tell how man should relate to Him. Secondly, because only the Creator can tell him how he should relate to himself, to other human beings, and to all other things in the universe. And, finally, because only God can give man a guidance which will be applicable universally, and for all times.

Say: Is there any of those you associate [with God] who guides to the Truth? Say: Only God guides to the Truth. Thus, then, He who guides to the Truth deserves more to be followed or He who cannot guide unless he be guided? What ails you? How judge you? And most of them follow nothing but conjecture, and conjecture can never take the place of truth (Yūnus 10: 35–6).

Say: Shall we call, apart from God, on that which neither benefits us nor harms us, and shall we be turned back on our heels after God has guided us aright? – Like one lured to bewilderment on the earth by Satans, and he has friends who call him to guidance: Come to us! Say: God's guidance is the only [true] guidance; and so we have been commanded to surrender to the Lord of all the worlds (al-An'ām 6: 71).

This, then, is the Divine law for the judgement of man. Central to this law is that the Truth be witnessed before mankind fully, faithfully, and by all possible means. For without guidance from God, man's earthly life, both individual and collective, will result in misery and suffering. But, more importantly, without that guidance man will never be in a position to make his ultimate destiny glorious.*

2. *God's promise to guide*: Adam, according to the Qur'ān, is neither a mythical figure nor merely a symbol of the human race. He is mentioned, as a Messenger, along with Noah and Abraham.

---

* For a more detailed discussion of the epistemological position, see Sayyid Mawdudi's *Let Us Be Muslims* (Leicester, 1985, pp. 119–23) and his forthcoming *Why Only the Divine Guidance*, to be published by the Islamic Foundation.

God chose Adam, and Noah, and the House of Abraham and the House of Imran above all mankind, offspring of one another (Āl 'Imrān 3: 33).

He was given knowledge and guidance (2: 31–5); when he erred and his weaknesses became known to him, God turned towards him in mercy, exhalted him, guided him and promised him and his progeny continuing guidance (20: 115–27, 2: 38–9).

Adam disobeyed his Lord, and so he erred. Thereafter his Lord chose him, and so He turned towards him, and He guided him. He said: Get you down, both of you, from here, each of you an enemy to each. Nonetheless, there shall most certainly come unto you guidance from Me; and he who follows My guidance shall not go astray, neither shall he be unprosperous. But whosoever turns away from My remembrance, his shall be a life of narrow scope; and on the Resurrection Day, We shall raise him blind. He shall say: O my Lord, why has Thou raised me blind, whereas I was given sight? God shall say: Thus it is. Our revelations came unto you and you did forget them; and so today you are forgotten (Ṭā Hā 20: 121–6).

3. *Messengers and their mission*: It was in fulfilment of this promise to mankind that, firstly, God sent His Messengers with His guidance, with the Truth, to every people – some of them the Qur'ān has named, some it has not.

We have sent you [O Prophet] with the Truth, as a bearer of glad tidings and a warner; not a community there is, but there has passed away in it a warner (al-Fāṭir 35: 24).

We have revealed to you [O Prophet] as We revealed to Noah and the Prophets after him, as We revealed to Abraham and Ishmael and Isaac and Jacob and their descendants, including Jesus and Job and Jonah and Aaron and Solomon, and as We gave to David Psalms; and Messengers We have mentioned to you before, and Messengers We have not mentioned to you; and as God spoke His word unto Moses. Messengers [We sent] as heralds of glad tidings and as warners, so that mankind might have no excuse before God after [the coming of] the Messengers; and God is All-mighty, All-wise (al-Nisā' 4: 163–5).

Secondly, He charged all of them with this mission and duty: to communicate the Truth, to invite people to worship the One God alone and surrender to Him as their only Lord – by word and example. In other words, to witness to the Truth before men and women to whom they were sent, so that they could have no plea to make before God, so that they could be questioned as to how they lived their lives, so that those who lived by the Truth could be rewarded, and those who did not could be punished.

> And We never sent, before you, any Messenger except that We revealed to him: There is no god but I; so serve and worship only Me (al-Anbiyā' 21: 25).

> And this was Our argument, which We gave to Abraham as against his people. We raise up in degrees whom We will; surely your Lord is All-wise, All-knowing. And We gave Isaac and Jacob, and both of them We guided – and Noah We guided before – and [We guided] of his descendants: David, and Solomon, and Job, and Joseph, and Moses, and Aaron – and thus do We reward the doers of good – Zachariah and John, and Jesus, and Elijah, each was of the righteous; and Ishmael, and Elisha, and Jonah, and Lut. And every one of them did We favour above other people. And [likewise We guided] some of their forefathers and their descendants and their brethren. And We elected them, and guided them onto the straight path. That is God's guidance; He guides by it whomsoever He wills of His servants. And had they ascribed partners [to God], in vain would have been all that they ever did. Those are they to whom We gave the Book, and the Judgement, and the Prophethood. So if these deny this [Our guidance], We have entrusted it to people who do not disbelieve in it. Those [Messengers] are they whom God has guided; follow, then, their guidance. Say: I ask of you no reward for it; it is but a reminder unto all mankind (al-An'ām 6: 83–90).

> Indeed We sent forth Our Messengers with clear revelations and We sent down with them the Book and the Balance, so that mankind may establish justice (al-Ḥadīd 57: 25).

The Prophet Muhammad was the last of them. He did not bring any new Truth, message or guidance; he came with the same Truth, and was entrusted with the same mission and duty as were all the Messengers preceding him. This duty and mission has been expressed in a number of ways: warning (*indhār*), bringing glad

58

tidings (*tabshīr*), inviting and calling (*da'wah*), communicating (*tablīgh*), reminding (*dhikr*), teaching (*ta'līm*), conveying and propagating (*tilāwah*), enjoining and promoting what is good and right and forbidding and eradicating what is wrong and bad (*amr bi 'l-ma'rūf wa nahī 'ani 'l-munkar*), establishing Din (*iqāmah*), establishing justice (*qist*), making the Divine guidance and Din prevail (*izhār*), or witnessing (*shahādah*). All these expressions pertain to the same mission, though from different perspectives and with different emphases.

> O Prophet, We have sent you as a witness [to the Truth], and as a herald of glad tidings and a warner, and as one who calls to God, by His leave, and as a light-giving lamp (al-Aḥzāb 33: 45–6).

> O Messenger, deliver that which has been sent down to you from your Lord; for if you do not, you will not have delivered His message (al-Mā'idah 5: 67).

> Even so We have sent among you, of yourselves, a Messenger, to convey unto you Our revelations, and to purify you, and to teach you the Book and wisdom, and to teach you that which you knew not (al-Baqarah 2: 151).

> It is He who has sent forth His Messenger with the guidance and the way of the Truth, so that he makes it prevail over all other ways of life; and God suffices as a witness (al-Fatḥ 48: 28; also 9: 33, 61: 9).

> . . . and those [among the followers of Moses] who follow the Messenger, the unlettered Prophet, whom they find written down with them in the Torah and the Gospel, who will enjoin upon them the right and forbid them the wrong, and make lawful to them the good things and make unlawful for them the bad things, and lift from them their burdens and the shackles that were upon them. Those who believe in him and succour him and help him, and follow the light that has been sent down with him – it is they who are the prosperous (al-A'rāf 7: 157).

4. *Man's accountability and the witness*: The witness given by the Messengers, and by all those who are charged with the same duty, is the basis for man's accountability in the *Ākhirah*, and his consequent reward and punishment. The Truth is witnessed before them so that they are left with no argument against God; they will be charged because they received it: this position has been stated

in the Qur'ān in many places and from many different perspectives, as we have seen before.

> Whoever follows the right path, follows it for his own good, and whoever goes astray, goes astray to his own loss; and no bearer of burdens shall bear the burden of another. We never chastise, until we have sent forth a Messenger (al-Isrā' 17: 15).

> So, [on Judgement Day,] We shall most certainly call to account all those unto whom [Our] message was sent, and We shall most certainly call to account the Message-bearers; and thereupon We shall most certainly relate unto them [their account] with knowledge, for We were never absent (al-A'rāf 7: 6–7).

> And when We took a pledge from all the Prophets – from you [O Prophet], and from Noah, and Abraham, and Moses, and Jesus, the son of Mary – We took from them a solemn pledge, so that He might question the truthful concerning their truthfulness, and He has prepared for those who deny the truth a painful punishment (al-Aḥzāb 33: 7–8).

> The day when God shall assemble all the Messengers, and say: What answer were you given? They shall say: We have no knowledge; Thou art the Knower of the things unseen (al-Mā'idah 5: 109).

> [And God will say:] O community of jinn and men, did not Messengers come unto you from among you, who conveyed unto you My revelations and warned you of the meeting of this your day? They shall say: We bear witness against ourselves. They were deluded by the life of this world, and they bear witness against themselves that they had been disbelievers (al-An'ām 6: 130).

> Then the disbelievers shall be driven in companies into Jahannam till, when they reach it, its gates will be opened, and its keepers will say to them: Did not Messengers come to you, from among yourselves, who conveyed unto you your Lord's revelations, and warn you against the meeting of this your Day? They shall say: Yes, indeed! But the word of punishment will have fallen due upon the disbelievers; and it shall be said to them: Enter the gates of Jahannam, to dwell therein forever. How evil is the abode of those who are arrogant! (al-Zumar 39: 71–2).

Surely We shall help Our Messengers and those who have believed, in this world's life and on the Day when all the witnesses shall stand up – the day when their excuses shall not profit the evil-doers, and theirs shall be the curse, and theirs the evil abode (Ghāfir 40: 51–2).

5. *Sense of responsibility*: The Qur'ān gives a very moving account of how God's Messengers devoted themselves in all earnestness to their mission, how they laboured hard to fulfil their duty, how they suffered heavily in their cause. Their history is ample testimony of this. But here two examples should suffice: firstly, that of the Prophet Noah and secondly, that of the Prophet Muhammad, blessings and peace be on them.

Indeed, We sent Noah unto his people, and he dwelt among them a thousand years, all but fifty . . . (al-'Ankabūt 29: 14).

He [Noah] said: My Lord, I have been calling my people night and day, but my call has only caused them to flee farther away. And whenever I called them, that Thou mightest forgive them, they put their fingers in their ears, and wrapped themselves in their garments, and persisted, and became arrogant in their pride. Then indeed I called them openly, then indeed I spoke publicly unto them, and I spoke unto them in private (Nūḥ 71: 5–9).

Would you [O Prophet], perhaps, torment yourself to death because they refuse to believe? (al-Shu'arā' 26: 3).

6. *Types of witness*: The witness by word may be taken to be broadly subsumed under the Quranic terminology of warning (*indhār*), bringing glad tidings (*tabshīr*), inviting and calling (*da'wah*), communicating (*tablīgh*), teaching and instructing (*ta'līm*), conveying and propagating (*tilāwah*). The terminology for the witness by actions includes establishing Islam (*iqāmatu 'd-dīn*), making God's guidance and way of life prevail over all others (*iẓhār*), establishing justice (*qist*), enjoining right and forbidding wrong, and Jihad.

7. *Consequences of failure and neglect*: The mission to witness the Truth and invite mankind to surrender to its Creator has the status of a covenant with God. Those who give up this mission, or fail to fulfil it or neglect it, are guilty of breaching their covenant. Hence they are cursed by God, and deprived of His blessings. They are cursed by angels, too, because the light brought by them

has been extinguished by such people while mankind gropes in darkness; and by mankind as well, for its sufferings and miseries are due mainly to the conduct of those who were entrusted with that light.

> Those who conceal the clear messages and the guidance that We have sent down, after We have made them clear, for mankind, in the Book – they shall be cursed by God and the cursers; but such as repent and put themselves right, and make [the Book] known – towards them I shall turn, I am the Accepter of repentance, the Mercy-giving. But those who remain [in the state of] denial and die denying – upon them shall be the curse of God, and the angels, and of all mankind . . . (al-Baqarah 2: 159–61).

> And, humiliation and powerlessness afflicted them, and they earned God's anger; all this, because they persisted in denying God's messages and in slaying the Prophets against all right; all this, because they rebelled [against God], and persisted in transgressing [the bounds of God] (al-Baqarah 2: 61).

The duty, obviously, is neglected or given up for the sake of worldly gains. These gains the Qur'ān describes as a trifle, which earn God's anger for the defaulters. The punishment for this crime, which the Qur'ān mentions, is indeed the only one of its kind, for such punishment is not mentioned for any other crime.

> Indeed, those who conceal what God has sent down in the Book, and barter it away for a trifle price – they eat nothing but fire in their bellies. And God shall not speak unto them on the Day of Resurrection, nor purify them; and for them is painful punishment. It is they who have bought error at the price of guidance, and punishment at the price of forgiveness. How patiently have they accepted the Fire! All that, because God has sent down the Book with the Truth, those who differ in the matter of the Book are most deeply in the wrong (al-Baqarah 2: 174–6; also 3: 77–8).

8. *The Jewish example*: The history of the people of Israel is narrated by the Qur'ān in considerable detail. It provides the most instructive example of a people who were guided by some of the greatest Messengers of God. They made a covenant with God that they will be only His servants and obey only Him and be His witnesses. They rose to great heights and contributed much to the

good of mankind by fulfilling their covenant. But, finally, they broke their covenant, suffered grievously, and thus became an object lesson in how people chosen by God to be witnesses to His guidance may go astray and how they may earn God's anger.

The purpose of narrating their history is neither to create hatred against any particular religion and people nor to take pleasure and comfort in their suffering and humiliation. This becomes evident from the fact that, despite very severe strictures against the people of Israel by the Qur'ān, the most peaceful and glorious days of Jewish history, in the last two thousand years, have been lived under Islamic rule. In fact their history is meant to act like a mirror which the Qur'ān holds to the Muslims so that they may recognize themselves when they go astray and may remain aware of the painful consequences of such conduct. Another purpose, of course, was to awaken the Jews at the time of the Prophet, blessings and peace be on him, and to invite them to believe in the Last Prophet and support him, as their own mission demanded. The Quranic account is similar to the Biblical account; if anything, much milder in tone and language.

Firstly, the Qur'ān shows that great blessings were conferred by God on the people of Israel, the greatest of them being the Book and guidance from Him, and that they were chosen to be His special servants.

Children of Israel, remember My blessing with which I blessed you, and how I favoured you above all other people (al-Baqarah 2: 47).

And when Moses said unto his people: O my people, remember God's blessing upon you, when He appointed among you Prophets, and made you kings, and gave you such as He had not given to any beings (al-Mā'idah 5: 20).

And when We made a covenant with the Children of Israel: You shall serve and worship none but God; and to be good to parents, and the near kinsman, and to the orphan, and to the needy; and speak good to man, and perform the prayer, and give the alms (al-Baqarah 2: 83).

And when We made covenant with you [O Children of Israel], and raised above you the Mount: hold fast with [all your] strength unto what We have given you, and remember what is in it, so that you might remain conscious of God. Then you turned away after that . . . (al-Baqarah 2: 63–4).

> Surely We sent down the Torah, wherein was guidance and light; thereby the Prophets, who had surrendered themselves [to God], gave judgement for those who were Jews; and so did the men of God and the rabbis, following such portion of God's Book as they were given to keep; and they bore witness to its truth (al-Mā'idah 5: 44).

The Bible gives a similar account:

> Do this because you belong to the Lord your God. From all the peoples on earth, He chose you to be His own special people. The Lord did not love you and choose you because you outnumbered other peoples; you were the smallest nation on earth (Deut. 7: 6–7).

> At Mount Sinai the Lord our God made a covenant, not only with our fathers, but with all of us who are living today. There on the mountain the Lord spoke to you face-to-face from the Fire . . . The Lord said, 'I am the Lord your God, who rescued you from Egypt, where you were slaves. Worship no god but Me' (Deut. 5: 2–7).

> Israel, remember this! The Lord – and the Lord alone – is our God. Love the Lord your God with all your heart, with all your soul, and with all your strength. Never forget these commands that I am giving you today. Teach them to your children. Repeat them when you are at home and when you are away, when you are resting and when you are working. Tie them on your arms and wear them on your foreheads as a reminder. Write them on the door-posts of your houses and on your gates (Deut. 6: 4–9). [This is a very good exegesis of the Quranic words 'and remember'.]

> Never forget the Lord your God or turn to other gods to worship and serve them. If you do, then I warn you today that you will certainly be destroyed (Deut. 8: 19).

> People of Israel, you are My witnesses; I chose you to be My servant, so that you would know Me and believe in Me and understand that I am the only God. Beside Me there is no other god; there never was and never will be (Isa. 43: 10).

Secondly, the Qur'ān exhorts and invites the people of Israel, as does the Bible, to fulfil their covenant with God, to believe in His last message, and to bear witness to its truth, reminding them of the promise and threat that were made to them.

Children of Israel, remember My blessing with which I blessed you, and fulfil My covenant [with you], and I shall fulfil your covenant [with Me]; and of Me alone stand in awe! (al-Baqarah 2: 40).

Remember that the Lord your God is the only God and that He is faithful. He will keep His covenant and show His constant love to a thousand generations of those who love Him and obey His commands, but He will not hesitate to punish those who hate Him (Deut. 7: 9–10).

If you obey the Lord your God and do everything He commands, He will make you His own people, as He has promised . . . The Lord your God will make you the leader among the nations and not a follower; you will always prosper and never fail . . . But if you disobey the Lord your God and do not faithfully keep all His commandments and laws that I am giving you today, all these evil things will happen to you . . . the Lord will curse everything you do . . . (Deut. 28: 9–19).

I will be your God, and you will be My people (Lev. 26: 12).

Thirdly, the Qur'ān indicts the people of Israel for breaking their covenant and neglecting their duty to worship and obey only God and to be His witnesses. Not only did they themselves turn away from the message of their Lord, they also prevented others from accepting and following it.

People of the Book, why do you disbelieve God's revelations while you yourselves witness [their truth]? People of the Book, why do you cloak the truth with falsehood and conceal the truth, and that knowingly (Āl 'Imrān 3: 70–1).

Say: People of the book, why do you bar from the path of God those who believe, trying to make it appear crooked, you yourselves being witnesses to its truth? (Āl 'Imrān 3: 99).

Indeed, God made covenant with the Children of Israel, when We raised from among them twelve of their leaders, and God said: I am with you. Surely, if you perform the prayer, and pay the alms, and believe in My Messengers, and succour them and lend to God a good loan, I will surely efface your evil deeds and I will admit you to gardens through which running waters flow. But whosoever of you thereafter disbelieves, surely he has gone astray from the right way.

Then, for their breaking their covenant We cursed them and made their hearts hard . . . (al-Mā'idah 5: 12–13).

Indeed, We made covenant with the Children of Israel, and We sent Messengers to them; whenever there came to them a Messenger with what they did not like [they rebelled], to some they gave the lie, while others they slayed (al-Mā'idah 5: 70).

The People of the Book will ask you to bring down upon them a Book from heaven; and they asked Moses for greater than that, for they said: Make us see God face to face – whereupon the thunderbolt overtook them for their evil doing. Then, they took to [worshipping] the calf – and this after the clear Truth had come to them; yet We pardoned them that, and We bestowed upon Moses a clear authority [for the Truth]. And We raised above them the Mount, making covenant with them; and We said to them: Enter the gate, prostrating; and We said to them: Transgress not the Sabbath; and We made a solemn covenant with them. So, [We cursed them] for their breaking the covenant, and their denying the revelations of God, and their slaying the Prophets without right, and for their saying, 'Our hearts are closed [to false guidance]' – nay, but God sealed them for their disbelief, so they believe not, except a few – and for their disbelief, and their uttering against Mary an awesome calumny, and for their saying, 'We killed the Messiah, Jesus, son of Mary, the Messenger of God' (al-Nisā' 4: 153–7).

Cursed were the disbelievers among the Children of Israel by the tongue of David, and Jesus, the son of Mary; this, because they rebelled [against God] and persisted in transgression. They did not prevent one another from the wrongs they committed. Surely evil were the things they did (al-Mā'idah 5: 78–9).

The Bible speaks in the same vein. Its indictment is no different from that which the Qur'ān says, although it is said more harshly and with severer strictures.

In addition, the leaders of Judah, the priests, and the people followed the sinful example of the nations round them in worshipping idols, and so they defiled the Temple, which the Lord Himself had made holy. The Lord, the God of their ancestors, had continued to send prophets to warn His people, because He wanted to spare them and the Temple. But they ridiculed God's Messengers, ignoring His words and laughing at His prophets, until at last the Lord's anger against His people was so great that there was no escape (2 Chr. 36: 14–16).

God told me to write down in a Book what the people are like, so that there would be a permanent record of how evil they are. They are always rebelling against God, always lying, always refusing to listen to the Lord's teachings. They tell the prophets to keep quiet. They say: 'Don't talk to us about what's right. Tell us what we want to hear. Let us keep our illusions. Get out of our way and stop blocking our path. We don't want to hear about your holy God of Israel' (Isa. 30: 8–11).

But Your people rebelled and disobeyed You; they turned their backs on Your law. They killed the prophets who warned them, who told them to turn back to You. They insulted You time after time, so You let their enemies conquer and rule them (Neh. 9: 26–7).

The Children I brought up have rebelled against Me. Cattle know who owns them, and donkeys know where their master feeds them. But that is more than my people Israel know. They don't understand at all . . . The city that once was faithful is behaving like a whore! At one time it was filled with righteous men, 'but now only murderers remain. Jerusalem, you were once like silver, but now you are worthless; . . . Your leaders are rebels and friends of thieves; they are always accepting gifts and bribes. They never defend orphans in court or listen when widows present their case (Isa. 1: 2–23).

And this is how Jesus censures the people of Israel.

Jerusalem, Jerusalem! You kill the prophets and stone the Messengers God has sent you! . . . And so your temple will be abandoned and empty (Mt. 23: 37–8).

They tie on to people's backs loads that are heavy and are hard to carry, yet they aren't willing even to lift a finger to help them carry those loads. They do everything so that people will see them. Look at the straps with Scripture verses on them which they wear on their foreheads and arms, and notice how large they are! Notice also how long are the tassels on their cloaks! They love the best places at feasts and the reserved seats in the synagogues; they love to be greeted with respect in the market places and to be called 'Teacher' . . . You hypocrites! You lock the door to the Kingdom of heaven in people's faces, and you yourselves don't go in, nor do you allow in those who are trying to enter! . . . You clean the outside of your cup and plate, while the inside is full of what you have obtained by violence and selfishness . . . You are like whitewashed tombs, which look fine on the outside but are full of bones and decaying corpses on the inside . . . So you actually admit that you are the descendants of those who murdered the prophets! Go on, then, and finish what your ancestors started! You snakes and sons of snakes! How do you expect to escape from being condemned to hell? And so I tell you that I will send you prophets and wise men and teachers; you will kill some of them, crucify others, and whip others in the synagogues and chase them from town to town (Mt. 23: 4–34).

Perhaps the most moving account of the fate of Israel is in the lamentations of the Prophet Isaiah, peace be upon him. Describing Israel as a vineyard planted by God, he first describes how He blessed it with every bounty, then goes on to describe how it produced sour fruits, and how God punished it – something very similar to what Sayyid Mawdudi has said about the Muslims.

My friend had a vineyard
   on a very fertile hill.
He dug the soil and cleared it of stones;
   he planted the finest vines.
He built a tower to guard them,
   dug a pit for treading the grapes.
He waited for the grapes to ripen,
   but every grape was sour.

So now my friend says: 'You people who live in Jerusalem and Judah, judge, between my vineyard and me. Is there anything I failed to do for it? Then why did it produce sour grapes and not the good grapes I expected?

This is what I am going to do to my vineyard; I will take away the hedge round it, break down the wall that protects it, and let wild animals eat it and trample it down. I will let it be overgrown with weeds. I will not prune the vines or hoe the ground; instead I will let briers and thorns cover it. I will even forbid the clouds to let rain fall upon it (Isa. 5: 1–6).

Finally, the Qur'ān also makes it clear that, after Israel, it is the Muslims who have been appointed to fulfil the same mission as was granted to Israel.

> Indeed, We gave the Children of Israel the Book, the Judgement, and the Prophethood; and We provided them with good things, and We favoured them above all other people. And We gave them clear revelations pertaining to the affair [of their Din]; so they did not take to different ways – after the knowledge had come to them – except for the sake of mutual transgression . . . then We set you [O Muhammad] on the Way [Shari'ah] pertaining to the affair [of your Din]; therefore follow it, and follow not the likes and dislikes of those who do not know (al-Jāthiyah 45: 16–18).

9. *Illusions and excuses*: When a faith as total, pervasive, deep and dynamic as Islam – living in surrender to the One God – which is a calling and a commitment, becomes transformed into a religion, hereditary and sectarian, its followers invent certain popular beliefs to calm and quieten their conscience. On the basis of such illusions and excuses, they are able to live peacefully while failing in their total commitment to God. They neglect the mission that He has entrusted to them, as well as refuse to accept any summons to renew their faith and take up their duty. The Qur'ān mentions some such popular notions which had become part of the Jewish faith, and categorically rejects them. Again, the objective is neither to condemn a certain faith and people for all times to come nor to nurture hatred against them, but to induce them to correct their wrong beliefs, and more importantly, to warn the Muslims to beware of such notions. It is ironic that one would find all such popular beliefs to be part of the Muslims' faith as well today; for example, that our Ummah is the beloved of God, that Muslims, whatever the state of their belief and conduct, have a monopoly over Paradise, that God's mercies and rewards are reserved exclusively for them, that, even if they are punished, their punishment will last only a few days.

> And the Jews and Christians say: We are God's children, and His beloved ones. Say: Why then does He punish you for your sins? Nay, you are but human beings of His creating. He forgives whom He wills, and He punishes whom He wills (al-Mā'idah 5: 18).

And that they say: None shall enter Paradise unless he be a Jew or a Christian. Such are their wishful beliefs! Say: Produce your proof, if what you say is true! Nay, whosoever surrenders his whole being unto God, attaining to excellence, his reward shall be with his Lord, and no fear shall be on them, neither shall they sorrow (al-Baqarah 2: 111–12).

And they say: The Fire shall not touch us save a number of days. Say: Have you made with God a covenant – then God will not fail in His covenant – or you attribute to God some thing of which you know nothing? Not so; whoso earns evil, and is engulfed by his transgressions – those are the inhabitants of the Fire . . . (al-Baqarah 2: 80–1).

And when they are told: Believe in what God has sent down, they say: We believe in what was sent down on us; and they disbelieve what is beyond that, yet it is the truth confirming what is with them. Say: Why then did you kill God's Prophets in former times, if you were believers? (al-Baqarah 2: 91).

Say: If the abode in the life-to-come is to be for you alone, to the exclusion of all other people, then long for that – if what you say is true! But never will they long for it, because of what their hands have sent ahead; God knows the evil-doers; . . . (al-Baqarah 2: 94–5).

Objections Against the Jama'at Islami

The objective and programme of the Jama'at Islami, being in accordance with the Qur'ān and the Sunnah, little did we expect that any Muslim would object to them. However, since we embarked upon this road, an unending stream of objections has been directed against us. I shall take up some of them here; not all of them are worthy of consideration, and not all of them can be dealt with in this talk.

A New Sect

Some people allege: Your Jama'at Islami is founding a new sect in Islam. These people perhaps do not understand the real factors that lead to the emergence of sects. On analysis, these factors can be grouped into four types.

One, making something part of Islam which is extraneous to it, and then claiming that this is the basis for differentiation between Iman and Kufr.

Two, giving an unduly important place, as against the Qur'ān and the Sunnah, to a specific teaching of Islam, and then making it a basis for schism.

Three, taking extremist positions on interpretive opinions, and labelling those who disagree as iniquitous, astray or Kafir.

Four, elevating a particular person, apart from a Prophet, to a religious office and position and making his acceptance the criteria of Iman. Or, to consider one's own party as having the sole monopoly of truth.

Tell me, now: Are we guilty of any of the above four conducts? We shall repent and correct ourselves as soon as

---

This is the concluding part of Sayyid Mawdudi's address.

we have been convincingly told of our mistake, for we want to establish Islam, and not to create a new sect. If, on the other hand, we have made no such error, why should we be indicted of establishing a new sect. Look at our position in all these respects.

One, we stand for the whole of Islam, the true Islam, we invite Muslims to practise all of it, and to witness to it. Similarly, we have gathered together on the basis of the whole of Islam, and not on any one or more of its particular teachings.

Two, we consider all schools of interpretation, which lie within the bounds of the Shari‘ah, to be on the right path. We recognize every person's right to follow any of these schools which satisfies him. Forming sects on the basis of any of these schools, in our view, is not permissible.

Three, we have made no undue claims for the position of our Jamā‘at; we claim no monopoly of truth. What we say is this: We realized our duty; therefore, we have formed an organization. Now we remind you of your duty; you are free to join us, to do your duty on your own or join any group which you find doing this duty.

Four, we make no undue claims for our leaders. This movement has not rallied people round any particular personality. Neither is a special religious office claimed for anyone, nor are his miracles and piety advertised, nor is personal devotion to him a necessary condition of participating in the Jamā‘at, nor are people invited to him.

Instead, we invite people to the ideal which is the objective of every Muslim's life, to the principles which constitute Islam. All those who join us have equal status as members of the Jamā‘at. These members elect someone as their Amir, not because he has any personal right to this office but because every organized work requires a head. This elected Amir can be removed from office, and any other person may be elected in his place. He is the Amir of only this Jamā‘at, and not of the whole Ummah. Only those who belong to the Jamā‘at are obliged to obey him. We have no such misconception that anyone who does not pledge allegiance to us will die the death of Ignorance.

Tell me, for God's sake, how, in view of the above, is it possible for us to turn into a new sect? How strange that those who accuse us of this crime are themselves guilty of doing everything which strengthens sectarianism: of recounting stories of miracles, foreknowledge and visions, of devotion to personalities, claims of religious offices for their leaders, polemics and quarrels on peripheral issues, and groupings round schools of interpretation.

What, then, irritates them? Not that which they blame us for. But, and let no one take offence if I speak truthfully, perhaps because we invite them to follow the true purpose of Islam. They do not seem to like this and also that we do our work by a method which exposes their faults.

Why a Separate Organization?

It is said: Do whatever you like, but why have you formed a separate organization, with a name of its own? Does this not create dissension in the Ummah? This very strange objection surprises me. They tolerate many organizations which are formed for worldly ends and which are modelled on capitalist-democratic and fascist patterns, for such ends as secular politics, un-Islamic education, and religious sectarianism. However, no sooner is an organization formed on Islamic principles and for purely Islamic work than they begin to smell the danger of disintegration. Perhaps, again, what annoys them is not the formation of an organization as such, but of an organization which is devoted to work for the true purposes of Islam.

Let me tell them this. We have been compelled to form this organization as a last resort. For years I have been calling upon Muslims to turn away from the wrong paths and to concentrate their efforts on the mission entrusted to them by God. If all the Muslims had accepted this call, all of them would have constituted one single organization, an organization which would have enjoyed the status of al-Jama'ah, at least in India. There would have been no need to form one more organization among Muslims. In the presence of such al-Jama'ah, forming a new organization would have been unthinkable, indeed impermissible. Or, even if one Muslim organization would have accepted to work for the fulfilment of this mission, we would have been only too happy to join it.

When, however, no one responded to our persistent call, we had no alternative but to organize those who understood their duty, and to initiate a collective struggle. May I ask now: What else we should have done if not formed this Jamā'at? If you deny the obligatory character of this duty, then give your arguments. If you do not deny it, then tell me if any of the existing associations and parties are discharging this duty? If not, why are you blaming the very people who have taken this task upon themselves?

Why Amir?

Some other critics say: Why have you employed the term 'Amir' for the leader of your Jamā'at? They contend, on the basis of certain Hadith, that only a person possessing the authority of state and the power of arms can be called 'Amir' or 'Imam'. Further, that only a leader in knowledge, in Prayer or in war, can legitimately be an Imam.

It appears that such critics know only that Fiqh and Hadith which pertain to the situation when Islam had attained full political power and possessed the power of arms. Unfortunately, what they do not seem to know are the injunctions dealing with the situation when political and military power has been wrested from Muslims, and when the organization of their society is in disarray. Would these critics care to tell us what course Muslims should adopt under the latter situation? Should they continue to live as individuals and hope and pray for the day when God would send an Imam, armed with power and authority, or should they struggle collectively to create such a power and authority? If collective

74

struggle is essential, can such struggle be carried out without forming an organization? If they agree that there is no alternative to forming an organization, do they imagine that an organization can function without a leader? If they admit this need too, will they tell us the Islamic terminology for such a leader? That terminology we are prepared to accept.

Otherwise, they should be honest enough to admit that, if their contention about Imamate is right, Islam gives us no guidance for a situation when Muslims are reduced to a state of powerlessness. Further, that anyone who wants to change their condition must follow un-Islamic methods and terminology. If they do not mean such preposterous propositions, and I hope they do not, then we are at a loss to understand why they should approve of terms such as President, Leader and Qa'id, but become enraged over the use of an Islamic term such as Amir. Some difficulty in understanding this issue arises because, in the beginning, the terms Amir and Imam were used when the Islamic state first came into existence. Prior to that, the Prophet, blessings and peace be on him, was himself leading the struggle to establish Islam, hence there was no need for such terminology in his time. But this is no reason to prohibit its use in our situation.

On examining all the teachings of Islam, it becomes evident that it enjoins organization in every collective activity. Such organization, it prescribes, should have a corporate structure, a system of communication and obedience within that structure, and a leader. For example, Islam lays down that the Prayer should be performed in congregation, which should have an Amir, that the Pilgrimage should be performed in an organized manner, again with an Amir. So much so that even if three persons go on a journey they should appoint one of them as their Amir. One Hadith lays down:

> When three persons set out on a journey, they should appoint one of them as their leader (*Abū Dā'ūd*, reported by Abū Sa'īd al-Khudrī).

75

Indeed, another Hadith goes even further:

> It is not lawful for three persons that they be in a wilderness and yet appoint not one of them as their leader (*Aḥmad*, reported by Abdullah Ibn Umar).

Thus, not only on a journey, but under all circumstances, Muslims must live an organized life and they should not undertake any collective activity without organizational structure and leadership. It is this spirit of Islam which Sayyidina Umar expressed as below:

> There is no Islam without *jamā'ah* (organization), and no *jamā'ah* without *imārah* (leadership), and no *imārah* without obedience (*Jāmi' Bayān al-'Ilm* by Ibn Abd al-Barr).

From all this we have concluded that an organization must be formed to strive to establish Islam (*iqāmah*) and witness to it, and that, it is in the fitness of things, that its leader should be called 'Amir'.

Collection of Zakah

Another strange objection runs like this. The leader of such a party has no right to collect Zakah, because only the Amir of an Islamic state has such a right. These critics probably have not tried to understand the system of our Zakah collection. We make no claim that *all* Muslims *must* deposit their Zakah in our Baytul Mal, nor do we claim that such Zakah as is not deposited in our Baytul Mal will not be lawfully paid. We only require that the members of our own Jamā'at pay their Zakah into the Jamā'at's Baytul Mal. By doing so, we only desire that Muslims should become used to the custom of collecting and expending Zakah on a collective level, as the Shari'ah desires them to do.

Now tell me what is wrong, from the viewpoint of the Shari'ah, in this policy and procedure? If we can ask people to perform their Prayer in congregation, and not in their homes, why can we not urge them to pay their Zakah under a collective system, rather than individually? Is it not strange that, while things like subscriptions, admission and member-ship fees, are considered to be right, only the procedure laid down by Allah and the Messenger is frowned upon as being impermissible?

Why Baytul Mal?

Another criticism runs like this. Why have you set up a Baytul Mal? Hearing such a ludicrous charge, one begins to wonder if these critics dislike the very terminology of Islam. Obviously, our Jamā'at like any other organization, has its own funds to meet its expenses. Our party funds are called Baytul Mal because it is an Islamic term. Ironically, had we called it 'treasury' or 'exchequer' the critics would have raised no objection, but would rather have been very pleased. What they find intolerable is that we have used an Islamic term for it!

I have not found it desirable to waste your time by replying to all the allegations against the Jamā'at, most of which are absurd. I have, however, taken up some of them only to show the type of excuses, criticisms, doubts, and allegations which are invented by those who neither want to do their duty nor let others do theirs. It shows how they prevent themselves, and others, from following the way of God.

Quarrelling and engaging in polemics is alien to the nature of our work. We are always prepared to explain ourselves to those who sincerely desire to understand us. We are also prepared to change if any of our policies and actions is proved to be in error. What we do not want is to join issue with those whose purpose is to entangle themselves in vexatious polemics.

Index

THE QURANIC VERSES

al-Isrā'
17:26   14
17:44   16
17:105   15

al-Kahf
18:7   53

Ṭā Hā
20:115–27   57
20:121–6   57

al-Anbiyā'
21:25   58
21:47   54

al-Ḥajj
22:18   17
22:77–8   20

al-Mu'minūn
23:115–16   54

al-Nūr
24:25   14

al-Shu'arā'
26:3   61

al-'Ankabūt
29:14   61

Luqmān
31:30   14

al-Aḥzāb
33:7–8   60
33:40   20
33:45–6   19, 59

Sabā'
34:28   19

al-Fāṭir
35:24   57
35:31   15

al-Zumar
39:71–2   60

Ghāfir
40:19   54
40:39–40   55
40:51–2   61

Fuṣṣilat
41:20–1   16

al-Dukhān
44:38–9   54
44:39   14

al-Jāthiyah
45:16–18   69
45:21–2   54
45:32   14

al-Fatḥ
48:28   59

al-Ḥujurāt
49:15   21

al-Dhāriyāt
51:56–7   53

al-Ḥadīd
57:25   58

al-Ṣaff
61:9   59

al-Mulk
67:2   53

Nūḥ
71:5–9   61